WITHOUT YES PROGRESSIVE ROCK WOULD HAVE
BUT IT WOULD HAVE BEEN COMPLETELY DIFFERENT.
YES HELPED PIONEER THE GENRE, SET THE TEMPLATE & THEN KEPT REINVENTING IT.
HERE ARE THE PEOPLE THAT MADE THE MAGIC HAPPEN & SOME OF THEIR BANDS.
THESE MAY NOT CONFORM TO TRADITIONAL CROSSWORD PUZZLE STANDARDS,
BUT NEITHER DOES PROG-ROCK! SO, WHO CARES? JUST HAVE FUN & PROG ON! YES?

PUZZLES

MABEL GREER'S TOYSHOP & THE SYN
CHRIS SQUIRE
BILLY SHERWOOD & OLIVER WAKEMAN
JON ANDERSON
BENOIT DAVID & JON DAVISON
TREVOR RABIN
STEVE HOWE
PETER BANKS & IGOR KHOROSHEV
RICK WAKEMAN
TONY KAYE
GEOFF DOWNES & TREVOR HORN
PATRICK MORAZ
ALAN WHITE
BILL BRUFORD
ANDERSON BRUFORD WAKEMAN HOWE
YOSO & CIRCA
BUGGLES & ASIA
ANDERSON RABIN AND WAKEMAN & TOURS
ALBUMS
SONGS

© 2018 AARON JOY
ISBN 978-1-387-71198-7

PRINTING/DISTRIBUTION BY LULU, INC.

COVER ART AN IMAGE BY THE AUTHOR, 2001

TO CONTACT OR BUY BOOKS
LULU.COM/ARONMATYAS
ARONMATYAS@HOTMAIL.COM
P.O. BOX 15382, PORTLAND, MAINE 04112
USA

TENOR

5. FINAL MGT DRUMMER
7. FOUNDING GUITARIST & LEAD SINGER OF SYN
8. GROUP ANDERSON IN BEFORE MGT
12. REUNION SYN ALBUM SQUIRE DISCOURAGED FANS FROM BUYING
14. MGT RECORDED FOR THIS FAMED RADIO DJ OR STEED FRIEND
17. MGT CO-FOUNDING DRUMMER
19. SYN & MGT BASSIST
21. SYN MEMBER WHO BECAME PHOTOGRAPHER
23. BANKS TOOK BRIEF HIATUS FROM MGT TO RECORD WITH THIS SQUIRE BAND
25. SQUIRE & BANKS LEFT SYN FOR THIS BAND
27. CANCELLED SYN REUNION TOUR
28. SYN REUNION ALBUM
32. MGT VOCALIST WHO JOINED YES
34. SYN GUITARIST WHO DIED IN 2016 OR ART FORM
35. KEYBOARDIST ON UNRELEASED SYN RECORDING & FINAL MGT LINE-UP
36. REUNION MGT JAZZ FUSION BASSIST
37. MGT SONGS INCLUDED ON THIS YES COMP ALBUM

BASS

1. YES GUITARIST IN REUNITED SYN
2. REUNITED MGT PRODUCED BY THIS YES MEMBER OR WORLD TRADE
3. MGT AFTER BECAME YES SIGNED TO THIS LABEL
5. 2009 SYN ALBUM
6. SYN SUPPORTED THIS GUITARIST IN LONDON
9. MGT CO-FOUNDING BASSIST
10. SYN MERGED WITH THIS BAND WHICH INCLUDED CHRIS SQUIRE
11. MGT MEMBER WHO SUGGESTED THEY CHANGE NAME TO YES
13. MGT SONG OPENING 1ST YES ALBUM
15. SYN MUSICIAN ON YES ALBUM TORMATO
16. REUNITED SYN PLANNED 1ST TOUR WITH THIS YES MEMBER SOLO GROUP
18. ORIGINAL BASSIST WITH SYN REUNION
19. MGT CO-FOUNDING GUITARIST & VOCALIST OR C.S. LEWIS
20. SYN GUITARIST WHO JOINED MGT
22. REUNITED SYN DID EXTENDED VERSION OF THIS YES SONG
24. SYN ROOTS IN THIS R&B BAND
26. MGT SONG ON 1ST YES ALBUM FEATURED IN MOVIE *BUFFALO 66*
28. MGT CO-FOUNDING DRUMMER AUDITIONED FOR THIS CHRIS SQUIRE GROUP
29. GROUP BRUFORD IN BEFORE MGT
30. 2016 MGT ALBUM OF EARLY RECORDINGS
31. LAST GIG AS MGT IN THIS BRITISH CITY
33. TWINS IN REUNITED SYN

THE SYN IS TO ONLY WINDOWSHOP AT MABEL GREER'S TOYSHOP

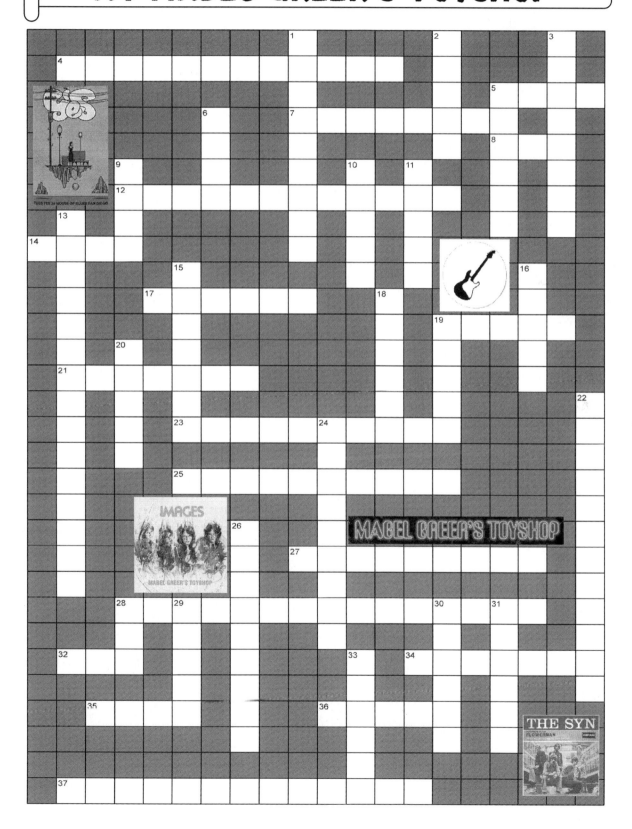

CHRIS SQUIRE

TENOR

4. XMAS ALBUM
7. NAMED (90125) CHRISSQUIRE
13. 1ST WIFE
14. MEMBER OF THIS GROUP WITH WHITE & JIMMY PAGE
16. SOLO BASS SONG FROM *FRAGILE* ALBUM
18. 2 ALBUMS WITH THIS SHERWOOD BAND
21. SUCCEEDED BY HIM IN YES AFTER DEATH
22. HIS 1ST BAND RECORDED THIS SONG BY THE WHO
23. 1ST PERFORMANCES WITH THIS TYPE OF MUSIC
26. YES SONG BRIEFLY QUOTED ON 1ST SOLO ALBUM
27. IN THIS BAND THAT INCLUDES WHITE & BANKS
28. SQUACKETT SONG ORIGINALLY WRITTEN FOR YES
29. CITED THIS AFRICAN AMERICAN BASSIST AS INFLUENCE OR MR. NORTON

BASS

1. INSTRUMENT BRAND
2. YES DRUMMER ON 1ST SOLO ALBUM
3. 2 SONGS BY CHRIS SQUIRE EXPERIMENT ON THIS YES ALBUM
5. YES KEYBOARDIST ON 1ST SOLO ALBUM
6. PROMO VIDEO FOR THIS SONG FROM 1ST SOLO ALBUM
8. 3RD WIFE OR COUNTRY
9. 1ST CONSPIRACY ALBUM ORIGINAL TITLE
10. DEATH FROM THIS ILLNESS
11. BAND FORMED BY 1ST WIFE WITH WHITE & HORN
12. AS HE CO-OWNS YES NAME THIS SPIN-OFF BAND WAS CREATED ABBREVIATION
15. SQUACKETT ALBUM
17. CONSPIRACY'S *I COULD* ALT VERSION OF THIS YES SONG
19. CHANGED HIS PLAYING STYLE TO SUIT THIS DRUMMER
20. NICKNAME
24. GUITARIST ON SOLO ALBUM & IN SQUACKETT
25. 2ND WIFE
27. 1ST ROCK BAND

CHRIS SQUIRE, R.I.P. THE FISH

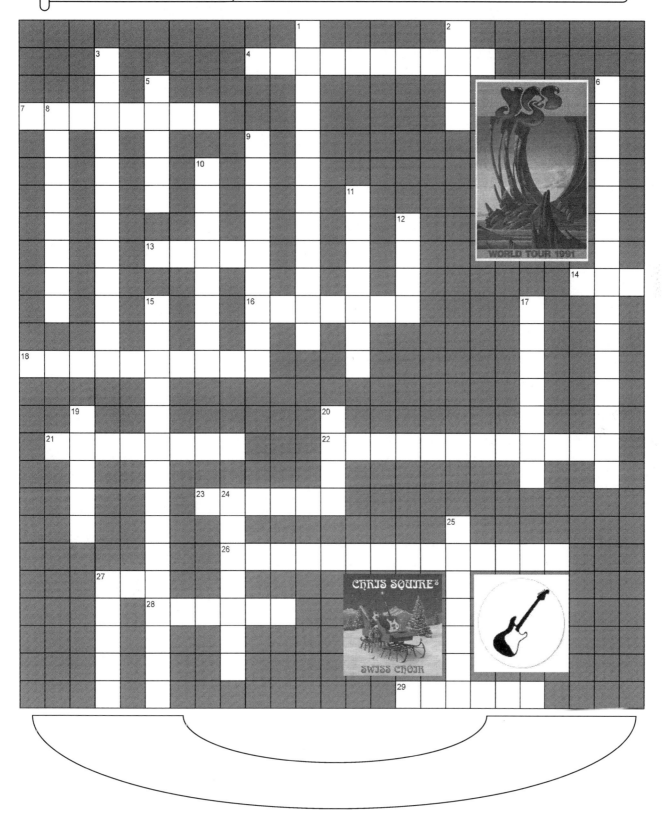

TENOR

1. WAKEMAN ON THIS 2005 HOWE ALBUM
5. WAKEMAN ON YES LIVE ALBUM *IN THE PRESENT* RECORDED HERE
6. SHERWOOD 1ST ALBUM WITH YES
7. WAKEMAN LEFT YES AFTER THIS TOUR
8. SHERWOOD LIVE ALBUM WITH YES
10. SHERWOOD GUEST ON THIS BAND'S ALBUM *KINGDOM OF DESIRE*
12. SHERWOOD & GUY ALLISON 2ND BAND
13. SHERWOOD INVOLVED WITH THIS SRV TRIBUTE ALBUM
15. WAKEMAN GUEST ON THIS AYREON PROJECT
16. SHERWOOD'S FATHER A MUSICIAN WHO APPEARED IN THIS 1957 FILM
18. WAKEMAN DID INCIDENTAL MUSIC FOR NUMEROUS ALBUMS WITH THIS ART FORM
22. WAKEMAN NOT ON THIS ALBUM BUT ON TOUR
24. GUITARIST WITH SHERWOOD IN LODGIC & CIRCA
25. SHERWOOD NOT JUST PERFORMED WITH YES BUT ALSO DID THIS WORK
26. SHERWOOD EARLY BAND WOULD INCLUDE THIS ASIA FEATURING JOHN PAYNE GUITARIST OR MASSACHUSETTS TATTOO ARTIST JOY
30. WAKEMAN JOINED THIS BAND THAT ONCE INCLUDED HIS FATHER
33. SHERWOOD GODFATHER
37. SHERWOOD INVOLVED WITH THIS QUEEN TRIBUTE ALBUM
38. WAKEMAN 1ST SOLO LIVE ALBUM RECORDED IN THIS COUNTRY
39. SHERWOOD & SQUIRE 2ND GROUP

BASS

1. SHERWOOD REJOINED YES BY REQUEST OF THIS MEMBER
2. WAKEMAN DISMISSED FROM YES WHILE RECORDING THIS YES ALBUM
3. SHERWOOD KEYBOARDS & GUITAR ON THIS YES ALBUM
4. WAKEMAN TO TOUR WITH YES FOR 40TH ANNIVERSARY BUT WAS ILL
9. WAKEMAN SUB KEYBOARDIST AT ROSFEST SHOW FOR THIS PROG BAND
11. SHERWOOD PRODUCED THIS JEFF BECK TRIBUTE ALBUM
14. SHERWOOD DEBUT SOLO ALBUM
17. WAKEMAN 1ST YES TOUR
19. WAKEMAN LIVE ALBUM *COMING TO TOWN* OF TOURS FOR THIS ALBUM
20. WAKEMAN DEBUT SOLO ALBUM
21. WAKEMAN 1ST ALBUM WITH PENDRAGON'S CLIVE NOLAN
23. WAKEMAN WON BEST KEYBOARD PLAYER AWARD NUMEROUS TIMES BY THIS SOCIETY
27. SHERWOOD & SQUIRE 1ST GROUP
28. VOCALIST ON WAKEMAN'S 1ST TOUR WITH YES
29. KEYBOARDIST REPLACING WAKEMAN IN YES
31. WAKEMAN ALBUM *HOUND OF THE BASKERVILLES* HAS THIS YES MEMBER
32. GUITARIST ON WAKEMAN ALBUM *RAVENS & LULLABIES*
34. SHERWOOD 1ST BAND WITH BROTHER WHO WORKED WITH AIR SUPPLY
35. HOWE ON THIS WAKEMAN 3 AGES SOLO ALBUM OR ALEISTER CROWLEY
36. SHERWOOD ORIGINALLY TO REPLACE THIS YES MEMBER

BILLY SHERWOOD'S FOREST IS WHERE YOU HEAR OLIVER WAKEMAN'S ALARM

jon anderson

TENOR

1. ALBUM OF VOICE & BIRD SONGS
3. COLLABORATOR WHO ALMOST REPLACED THIS KEYBOARDIST IN YES
8. 1ST YES ALBUM NOT TO FEATURE ANDERSON OR THEATER
9. EARLY DEMOS UNDER THIS NAME
11. SOLO BOX SET OF 20 ALBUMS
14. BAND ON THIS SOLO ALBUM WHILE ANDERSON APPEARS ON THEIR *THE SEVENTH ONE* ALBUM OR FAMED DOG
16. UNRELEASED SEQUEL TO *ANIMATION* ALBUM OR MODERNIST PAINTER
17. ANDERSON WAKEMAN ALBUM
20. *INVENTION OF KNOWLEDGE* ALBUM WITH THIS MUSICIAN
21. CONTRIBUTED TO ALBUM *CULTURE OF ASCENT* BY THIS PROG BAND
25. SONGS OF NEW EIRELAND ALBUM
26. NEW AGE COLLABORATOR
27. BAND ON *SONG OF SEVEN* ALBUM
28. ALBUM FEATURING CAMEOS FROM SOUTH AMERICAN MUSICIANS INCLUDING MILTON NASCIMENTO
29. 1ST BAND WHICH INCLUDED HIS BROTHER

BASS

2. EP OF A 20 MINUTE SONG OR NOT CLOSED
4. SON DAMION VOICE ON THIS YES SONG
5. SANG *SILVER TRAIN* & *CHRISTIE* FOR THIS BASSIST OR NAVAL COMMANDER
6. WORKING TITLE OF 2ND ABWH ALBUM
7. ON THIS KITARO ALBUM
10. NICKNAME WITH YES MEMBERS OR FAMED FRENCHMAN
12. ALBUM ORIGINALLY RELEASED AS *THE POWER OF SILENCE* BUT WITHOUT NARRATION
13. ALBUM RE-ISSUED AS JON & JANE ANDERSON
14. REMIX ALBUM
15. FINAL YES STUDIO ALBUM
18. TITLE CHARACTER OF DEBUT SOLO ALBUM
19. 1ST RECORDING
22. *BETTER LATE THAN NEVER* ALBUM WITH THIS BAND ABBREVIATION
23. JOINED THIS BAND WITH RABIN
24. ON ROCK SOUNDTRACK OF THIS SILENT FILM

THE REVEALING SCIENCE OF JON ANDERSON

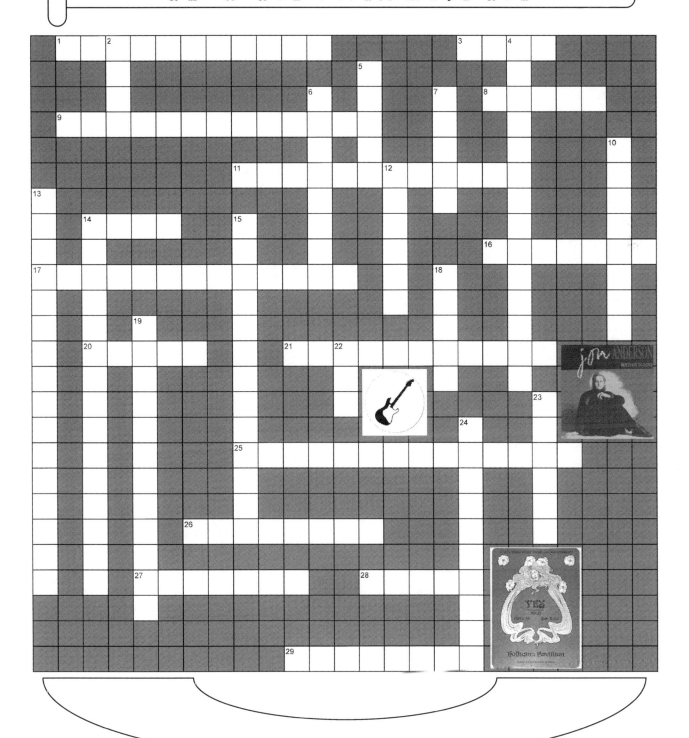

TENOR

2. DAVID REPLACED THIS YES MEMBER
4. ORIGINAL KEYBOARDIST ON DAVID'S ONLY STUDIO ALBUM WITH YES
9. DAVID FRONTED THIS BAND 1999 - 2013
10. 2011 LIVE YES ALBUM WITH DAVID
12. REPLACEMENT KEYBOARDIST ON DAVID'S ONLY STUDIO ALBUM WITH YES
13. DAVISON PERFORMANCE NICKNAME
14. DAVISON IN THIS YES TRIBUTE BAND
16. DAVISON STARTED SINGING IN THIS VENUE
17. DAVISON IN BANDS WITH TAYLOR HAWKINS OF THIS BAND OR NIRVANA ALUMNI
21. PRODUCER OF DAVISON'S 1ST STUDIO ALBUM WITH YES OR TOM & COLIN
22. PRODUCER OF DAVID'S ONLY STUDIO ALBUM WITH YES OR TOOT
27. SONG FROM *DRAMA* ON YES LIVE ALBUM WITH DAVID
28. SOME SONGS ON DAVID'S ONLY STUDIO ALBUM WITH YES HAD EARLIER LIFE WITH THIS BAND
29. DAVISON'S 1ST STUDIO ALBUM WITH YES IS HEAVEN & _____ (5)
30. WHILE LIVING IN BRAZIL DAVISON PLAYED WITH THIS POET OR REAGAN

BASS

1. DAVID IN THIS YES TRIBUTE BAND
3. DAVISON IS BASSIST & SINGER IN THIS SEATTLE PROG BAND
5. DAVID ON 2 ALBUMS BY THIS BAND
6. DAVISON ON THIS SHERWOOD SOLO ALBUM
7. 2ND YES LIVE ALBUM WITH DAVISON RECORDED HERE
8. YES STUDIO ALBUM BEFORE DAVID JOINED
11. DAVISON 1ST STUDIO ALBUM WITH YES ALSO LAST TO FEATURE THIS FOUNDING MEMBER
15. DAVISON ON THE *TALES FROM THE EDGE* YES TRIBUTE ALBUM WIH THIS BAND
18. DAVID ONLY STUDIO ALBUM WITH YES
19. ALBUM OF 1972 YES LIVE RECORDINGS RELEASED BETWEEN 2 LIVE YES ALBUMS WITH DAVISON
20. DAVISON IN THIS CHRISTIAN PROG BAND
23. DAVID'S ONLY LIVE ALBUM WITH YES ALSO ONLY YES ALBUM TO INCLUDE THIS KEYBOARDIST
24. DAVID'S LIVE ALBUM WITH YES RECORDED IN THIS COUNTRY
25. YES LIVE ALBUMS WITH DAVISON FEATURING FULL ALBUMS
26. DAVID HOME CANADIAN PROVINCE

BENOIT DAVID & JON DAVISON CRY OVER MARY

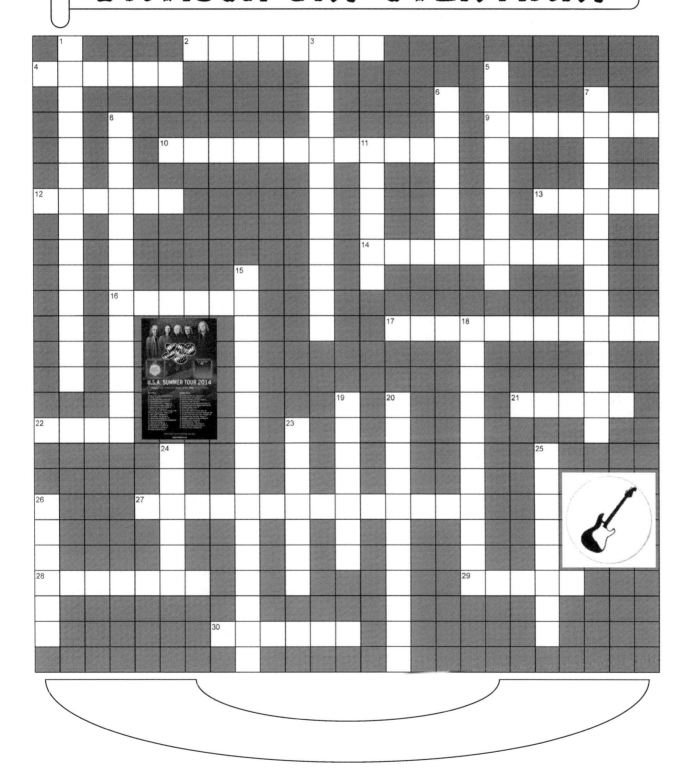

TENOR

4. HOME COUNTRY
8. WON THIS AWARD TWICE FOR RABBITT
12. FATHER PLAYED THIS INSTRUMENT
14. 1ST INSTRUMENT LEARNED
15. 2ND SOLO ALBUM
16. DECLINED TO TOUR WITH THIS CLASSIC ROCK BAND AS KEYBOARDIST
17. OWN L.A. RECORDING STUDIO
20. CO-PRODUCER OF 3RD SOLO ALBUM
24. 4TH SOLO ALBUM
25. PRODUCED DEBUT ALBUM BY THIS BAND WITH MEMBERS OF RAINBOW & THIN LIZZY OR ROLLING STONES PET
27. RABBITT CAME FROM THIS BAND
28. ON 2 ALBUMS BY HIS EARTH BAND

BASS

1. FINAL STUDIO ALBUM WITH YES
2. DEBUT SOLO ALBUM
3. RABBITT DEBUT ALBUM
5. 1ST HOLLYWOOD FILM SCORE
6. DEBUT SOLO ALBUM ORIGINALLY RELEASED AS THIS
7. ONLY SOLO LIVE ALBUM
8. TAUGHT THIS ACTOR GUITAR
9. 1ST FILM SCORED REISSUED AS THIS
10. LEGENDARY BASSIST ON 3RD SOLO ALBUM
11. ESTABLISHED THIS LABEL 1978
13. 3RD SOLO ALBUM
17. 1ST SINGLE BY RABBITT BY THIS BAND
18. ALMOST JOINED THIS SUPERGROUP WITH WAKEMAN & MEMBERS OF THIS SUPERGROUP
19. RABIN SQUIRE WHITE KAYE BAND
21. ONLY INSTRUMENT RABIN DIDN'T PLAY HIMSELF ON DEBUT SOLO ALBUM
22. 4TH SOLO ALBUM WRITTEN WITH A MEMBER OF THIS GROUP
23. STUDIED THIS MUSIC ROLE IN COLLEGE
26. A YEAR AFTER LEARNING GUITAR JOINED THIS BAND

WHAT IS TREVOR RABIN'S ZIP CODE?

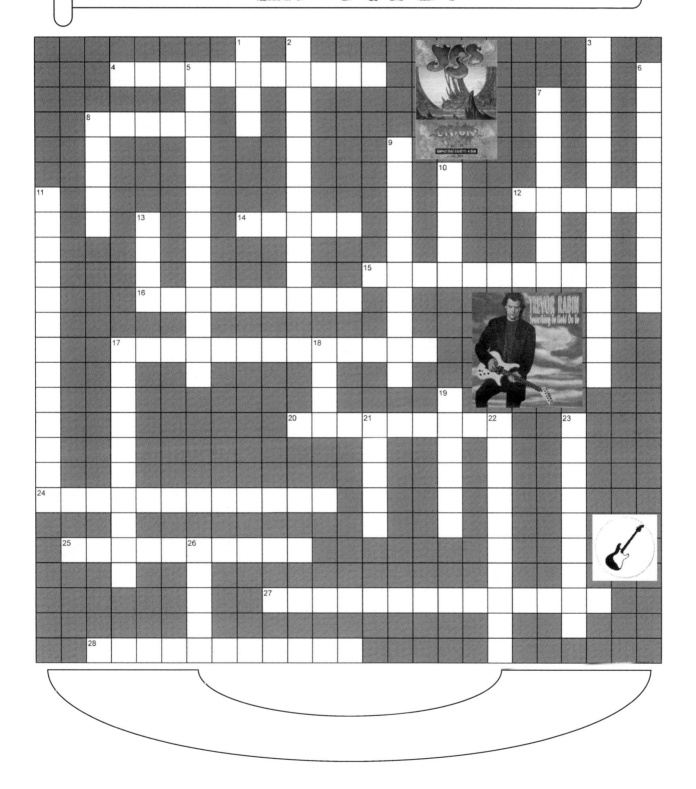

TENOR

2. 5 YRS IN A ROW VOTED BEST OVERALL GUITARIST BY THIS MAG
3. 1ST ALBUM WITH REUNITED ORIGINAL ASIA
4. CO-PRODUCED THIS ALBUM OF YES MUSIC
5. EARLY BAND TOMORROW ORIGINALLY RECORDED UNDER THIS NAME
12. REUNITED WITH ASIA ON THIS ALBUM
17. JAZZ TRIO WITH SON & ORGANIST ROSS STANLEY
18. DRUMMING SON PLAYED WITH THIS IAN DRURY GROUP
20. SON VIRGIL'S BAND
22. MULTI VOLUME SOLO ALBUM SERIES
23. DECLINED JOINING THIS KEITH EMERSON GROUP
24. DRUMMER ON *QUANTUM GUITAR* SOLO ALBUM OR BOB
25. GROUP WITH STEVE HACKETT
26. 1ST SOLO ALBUM
27. 1ST ALBUM WITH YES
28. 1ST RECORDINGS WITH THIS BAND

BASS

1. IN BAND THAT APPEARED IN MOVIE *SMASHING TIME* AS THE SNARKS OR WHEN
2. SIGNATURE MODEL GUITAR COMPANY
5. CONTRIBUTED TO THIS QUEEN SONG
6. LAST ALBUM WITH YES BEFORE 1981 DEPARTURE
7. FAMOUS FOR HAVING TRAINED IN THIS STYLE
8. 1ST WORKED WITH WAKEMAN RECORDING SOLO DEBUT OF THIS NYC SINGER-SONGWRITER OR NOT SQUEEZED
9. PICTURED ON THIS YES STUDIO ALBUM THAT DOES NOT INCLUDE HIM
10. YES KEYBOARDIST ON 1ST 2 SOLO ALBUMS
11. LEFT YES 2ND TIME AFTER THIS ALBUM
13. 3RD REUNION WITH YES ON THIS PAIR OF ALBUMS
14. EARLY BAND WHOSE ALBUM NOT RELEASED AS LABEL CLOSED
15. 1ST RECORDING
16. SUCCESSOR GUITARIST IN 1ST BAND & PREDECESSOR IN YES
19. DIET
21. HOWE WETTON PALMER DOWNES GROUP

ASK STEVE HOWE TO DO IT

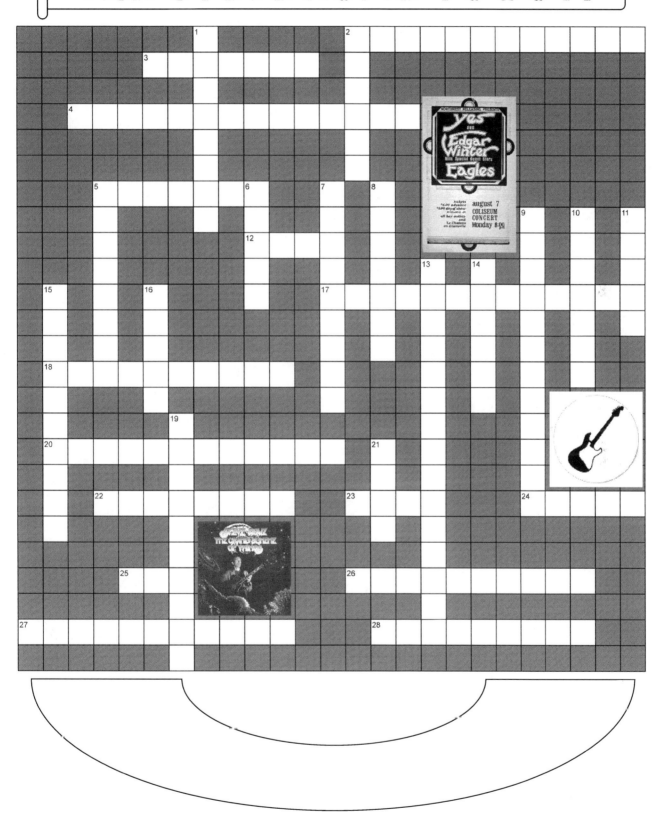

TENOR

5. BANKS 1ST RECORDINGS WITH THIS BAND
6. KHOROSHEV 2ND STUDIO ALBUM WITH YES
8. KHOROSHEV STUDIO ALBUM WITH YES HAS TRIBUTE TO THIS REGGAE MUSICIAN
9. BANKS 1ST STUDIO ALBUM WITH YES
11. BANKS COORDINATED THIS YES LIVE COMP
14. BANKS UNCREDITED GUITAR THIS LIONEL RITCHIE BALLAD
15. BANKS BAND FORMED WITH SQUIRE
18. KHOROSHEV 1ST STUDIO ALBUM WITH YES
24. BANKS 2ND STUDIO ALBUM WITH YES
26. KHOROSHEV COMPOSED MUSIC FOR THIS SOFTWARE
27. BANKS REAL LAST NAME
28. BANKS FORMED THIS BAND AFTER YES THAT INCLUDED GUEST KAYE OR GORDON
29. VIDEO GAME ASSOCIATED WITH KHOROSHEV'S 2ND STUDIO ALBUM WITH YES
30. BANKS SQUIRE KAYE ANDERSON BRUFORD BAND WITH SHERWOOD IN REUNION

BASS

1. ABANDONED KHOROSHEV & ANDERSON PROJECT
2. KHOROSHEV CO-PRODUCED THIS 2014 ALBUM WITH MIKE PLOTNIKOFF WHO WORKED WITH KISS
3. BANKS 1963 BAND OR TOM WAITS DINER
4. BANKS AFTER YES JOINED THIS BAND
7. ON TOUR KHOROSHEV PLAYED THIS INSTRUMENT IN ADDITION TO KEYBOARDS ON *ROUNDABOUT*
10. BANKS BAND WITH WIFE
12. KHOROSHEV ONLY LIVE ALBUM WITH YES ALSO LAST ALBUM FEATURING THIS MEMBER
13. KHOROSHEV LIVE ALBUM WITH YES
16. PRODUCER OF KHOROSHEV 1ST ALBUM WITH YES AS OFFICIAL MEMBER
17. KHOROSHEV ON 2 ALBUMS WITH CHARLIE FARREN OF THIS BAND
19. KHOROSHEV ON TRIBUTE ALBUM TO THIS PROG BAND ABBREVIATION
20. BANKS WAS SUCCESSOR TO HOWE IN THIS BAND
21. KHOROSHEV 1999 SOLO ALBUM
22. KHOROSHEV 1ST STUDIO ALBUM WITH YES ALSO 1ST ALBUM WITH THIS OTHER MEMBER
23. BANKS REPLACED THIS FUTURE IAN GILLAN BAND GUITARIST IN SYNDICATS
25. BANKS 1ST RECORDINGS INCLUDED *FOR YOUR LOVE* WHICH WAS HIT FOR THIS BAND

PETER BANKS ON IGOR KHOROSHEV'S RACING TIP

TENOR

8. REPLACED BY HIM AFTER 5TH REUNION IN YES
10. ANDERSON WAKEMAN ALBUM
11. KING JOHN & THE MAGNA CARTA
13. 1ST AUTOBIO
15. 1ST RECORDING SESSION FOR MEMBERS OF THIS DUO'S BAND
16. SOLO PIANO ALBUM ABOUT ISLE OF MAN
17. *THE PIANO ALBUM* REISSUE
20. DEVELOPED THIS INSTRUMENT WHILE WORKING WITH DAVID BOWIE
21. AT STRAWBS SHOW PUSHED THIS AVANT-GARDE ARTIST OFF STAGE NOT RECOGNIZING HIM
22. ON THIS OZZY OSBOURNE ALBUM
24. WROTE THIS SOLO CONNECTION ALBUM WITHOUT PLAYING ANY OF THE MUSIC
25. WHOSE 6 WIVES
27. ON SAME DAY WAS ASKED TO JOIN YES & HIS BAND
28. FINAL STRAWBS GIG FOR HIS RADIO SHOW OR EMMA
29. 2008 SOLO TOUR SHOW
30. SOLO EP OF MUSIC WRITTEN FOR FIREWORKS

BASS

1. UNOFFICIAL 1ST SOLO ALBUM THESE PIANO MOVEMENTS
2. *ASPIRANT SUNRISE* & *ASPIRANT SUNSET* & *ASPIRANT SUNSHADOWS*
3. 1ST SOLO NON-STUDIO ALBUM NOT TO CHART IN U.K.
4. ON THIS LOU REED ALBUM
5. TRILOGY OF NEW AGE SOLO ALBUMS ARE THESE OR PUTTING THIS ON
6. BORN IN THIS LONDON SUBURB OR *DOCTOR WHO'S* ACE HOME
7. HIS MYTHS & LEGENDS
9. EARLY NICKNAME
12. OWNS THIS CAR RENTAL COMPANY
14. ON THIS BLACK SABBATH SONG
18. WAKEMAN & WAKEMAN ALBUM ALIAS
19. MASONIC LODGE NAME
23. 1ST ALBUM WITH YES
26. ONLY 1990'S CHARTING SOLO ALBUM RETURNS HERE

JOURNEY WITH THE 6 WIVES OF RICK WAKEMAN

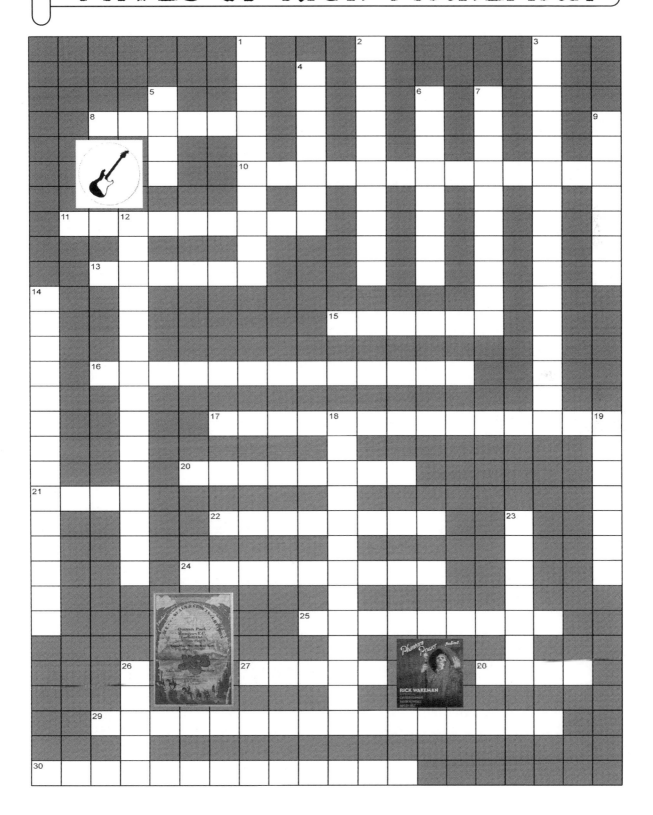

TENOR

1. TOURED WITH THIS FRENCH SINGER WHO HAS DONE OVER 181 TOURS
4. ABANDONED INSTRUMENTAL ALBUM RECORDED FOR THIS MAG
5. MEMBER OF THIS NEIL YOUNG TRIBUTE BAND
6. ENGAGED TO STEP-DAUGHTER OF THIS BASSIST
8. AUDITIONED FOR KEYBOARDIST ROLE IN THIS MOVIE
11. IN THIS BAND WITH WHITE & SHERWOOD
13. FOUNDED THIS BAND AFTER LEAVING YES 1ST TIME
17. HIS KEYBOARD PARTS RE-RECORDED FOR THIS YES ALBUM
19. BANKS SQUIRE ANDERSON BRUFORD KAYE BAND
20. 2 ALBUMS WITH THIS BAND WITH MICHAEL DES BARRES
21. FINAL ALBUM WITH YES
22. PLAYED THIS MUSIC TYPE IN DANNY ROGERS ORCH
26. ON RE-ISSUE OF THIS DAVID BOWIE ALBUM
27. TOURED WITH THIS SINGER 1975 - 1976
28. IN THIS BAND WITH SHERWOOD & BOBBY KIMBALL OF TOTO

BASS

2. 1ST RECORDED COMPOSITION
3. LAWSUIT AGAINST YES FOR THESE UNPAID
7. OFFERED TO STAY WITH YES NOT AS MUSICIAN BUT AS THIS
9. SONG ON YES ALBUM 9012*LIVE: THE SOLOS*
10. IN THIS BAND ORIGINALLY KNOWN AS IVEYS
12. ORIGINALLY KICKED OUT OF YES FOR PLAYING ONLY THIS INSTRUMENT
14. EARLIEST RECORDING
15. WITH THIS BANKS BAND FOR DEBUT BUT NOT OFFICIAL MEMBER
16. IN 2 BANDS WITH THIS GUITARIST WHO PLAYED ON YES ALBUM *UNION*
17. EARLIEST RECORDINGS WITH THIS BAND
18. SQUIRE WHITE RABIN KAYE BAND
22. 2ND TIME IN YES REPLACED BY THIS KEYBOARDIST WHO ALSO QUIT
23. ORIGINALLY REPLACED IN YES BY THIS KEYBOARDIST
24. OTHER KEYBOARDIST ON YES ALBUM *TALK*
25. RECORDED WITH THIS DOG BAND

TONY KAYE HAS A FLASHY BADFINGER

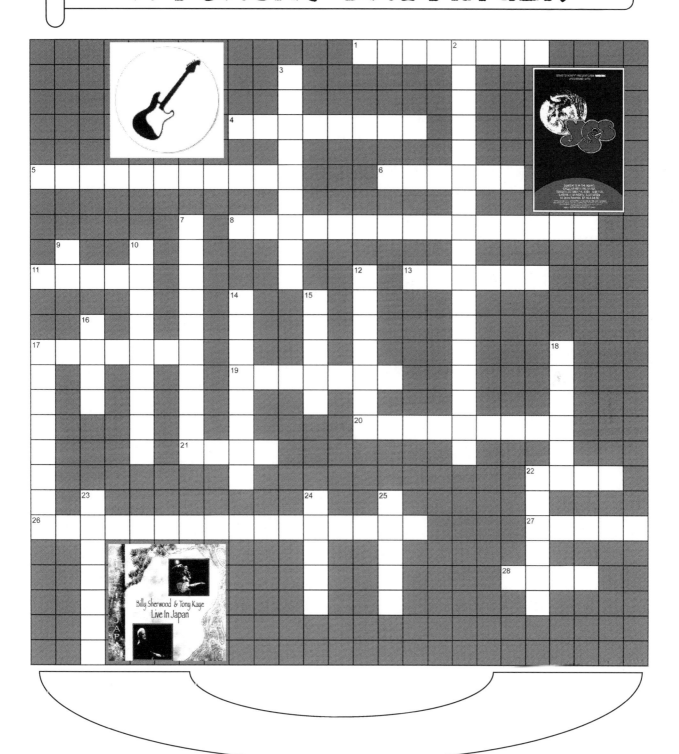

TENOR

1. BEFORE BUGGLES HORN RELEASED 2 SINGLES UNDER THIS NAME
4. DOWNES PRESENTED AWARD BY PRES OF THIS COUNTRY
5. 1ST DOWNES & HORN BAND
9. HORN FOUNDING MEMBER OF THIS NOISY SYNTH-POP BAND
11. DOWNES ON LIVE ALBUM BY THIS BAND WITH GLENN HUGHES
14. HORN PRODUCED HIS ALBUM *KINGS & QUEENS OF THE UNDERGROUND*
15. DOWNES JOINING CAUSED THIS BAND'S DEBUT ALBUM TO BE RE-RECORDED OR LENNON DRUMMER
16. DOWNES SUPERGROUP AFTER YES
18. DOWNES MET HORN WHILE AUDITIONING FOR HIM FOR THIS SINGER
21. HORN & DOWNES REUNITED WITH YES ON THIS ALBUM
24. DOWNES SOLO ALBUMS UNDER THIS ORCH NAME
25. TREVOR HORN BAND FORMED AS THIS
26. 1ST HORN & DOWNES ALBUM TOGETHER
27. HORN LEFT YES BEFORE FINISHING PRODUCTION ON THIS ALBUM
29. HORN 1ST GROUP

BASS

2. SONGWRITER WHO WORKED WITH HORN & DOWNES KNOWN FOR HIS SONGS BEING PERFORMED BY DANCE POP MUSICIANS
3. DOWNES WROTE YES SONG *WHITE CAR* INSPIRED BY THIS PERFORMER
6. BUGGLES HAD 1ST NUMBER ONE HIT FOR THIS LABEL
7. HORN MUSIC PUBLISHING COMPANY WITH WIFE
8. HORN INVOLVED WITH THIS BARRY MANILOW SINGLE
10. HORN PLAYED KEYBOARDS ON THIS PAUL MCCARTNEY ALBUM
11. HORN PRODUCED & WROTE FOR THIS RUSSIAN DUO
12. HORN 1ST INSTRUMENT
13. HORN & DOWNES BOTH JOINED YES VIA THIS ALBUM
17. HORN HIRED IAN DURY'S BACKING BAND TO RE-RECORD THIS SEXY FUTURE HIT
19. HORN SESSION MUSICIAN ON THIS TV SHOW
20. DOWNES & HORN BOTH COMPOSED THESE IN EARLY CAREERS OR JANE MANGINI AT BANG MUSIC
22. HORN & DOWNES JOINED YES VIA SHARING THIS MANAGER OR PENNY
23. DOWNES IN THIS BAND WITH MEMBER OF FIXX
28. DOWNES & JOHN WETTON OUTING

GEOFF DOWNES & TREVOR HORN CREATE TOO MUCH DRAMA

PATRICK MORAZ

TENOR

2. BEFORE MORAZ YES AUDITIONED THIS PIANIST WHO WOULD WORK WITH ANDERSON
3. INSTRUCTOR IN THIS
5. 2 ALBUMS WITH THIS YES DRUMMER
7. MORAZ RISTORI GRAHAM COCKETT BAND
8. BIRTH COUNTRY
11. LAST MOODY BLUES ALBUM
14. COMP OF TRACKS FROM 3 PIANO ALBUMS
19. AT 16 WAS YOUNGEST TO RECEIVE BEST SOLOIST AWARD AT THIS JAZZ FEST
22. DEBUT AS MOODY BLUES MEMBER VIA TOURING THIS ALBUM
23. REPLACED THIS KEYBOARDIST IN YES
24. ONLY MOODY BLUES SONG WRITTEN BY MORAZ PERFORMED BY THEM
26. ONLY STUDIO ALBUM WITH YES
27. ETUDES SONATAS & PRELUDES ALBUM
28. CONTRIBUTED WRITING THIS YES ALBUM
29. OPENER FOR EUROPEAN TOUR BY THIS JAZZ SAX PLAYER

BASS

1. PERFORMED PRIVATELY FOR THIS ARTIST
4. GUESTED ON THIS HOWE DEBUT SOLO ALBUM
6. TOURED JAPAN & HONG KONG AS MUSICAL DIRECTOR FOR THIS GROUP
9. 1ST MOVIE COMPOSITION
10. MOODY BLUES COMP ALBUM WITH EDITED BAND PHOTOS REMOVING MORAZ
12. FLAT FEE TOUR BOOKED BY FANS ABBREVIATION
13. MORAZ TRIO WITH NICE MEMBERS
14. FATHER WORKED FOR THIS CLASSICAL COMPOSER
15. 1ST ALBUM AFTER MOODY BLUES
16. PARTIALLY COMPOSED SOUNDTRACK TO THIS SCHWARZENEGGER MOVIE
17. GUEST ON THIS SQUIRE SOLO ALBUM
18. 2ND SOLO ALBUM
20. TOOK LESSONS FROM THIS JAZZ VIOLINIST
21. DEBUT SOLO ALBUM
25. PART OF THIS ROCK BAND IN BRAZIL

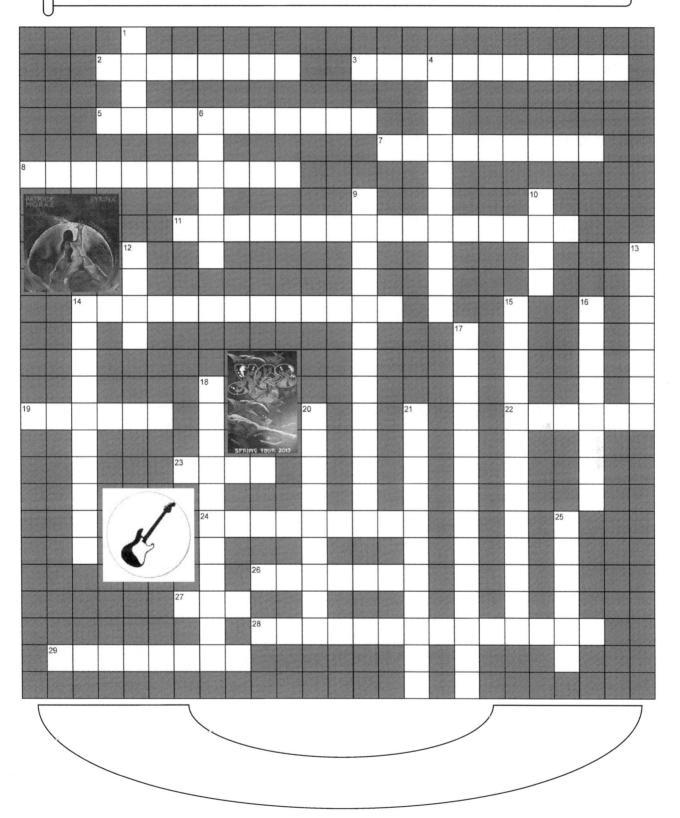

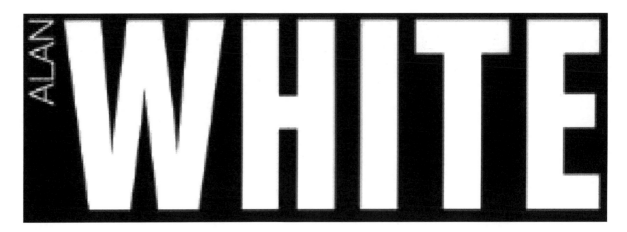

TENOR

5. TOURED WITH HIS BAND THE GAMBLERS
7. 1ST INSTRUMENT
9. 1ST STUDIO ALBUM WITH YES
10. 1ST SINGLE RELEASED
11. TOURED WITH THIS REUNITED PRE-YES SQUIRE BAND
17. 1ST GIG WITH PLASTIC ONO BAND
18. ONLY SOLO ALBUM
19. IN THIS BAND WITH WINGS GUITARIST DENNY LAINE
23. ON THIS GEORGE HARRISON ALBUM
24. TOURED WITH HIS AIR FORCE
25. GUITARIST ON HIS 1ST ALBUM WITH PLASTIC ONO BAND OR HE WAS HERE
27. PLANNED TO STUDY THIS IN COLLEGE
28. 1ST BAND
29. ON THIS SQUIRE SOLO ALBUM

BASS

1. YES KEYBOARDIST APPEARING IN PROMO FOR SOLO ALBUM BUT NOT ON ALBUM
2. MUSICIAN ON SOLO ALBUM ALSO ON HOWE SOLO DEBUT OR ABBOTT
3. PART OF THIS ABORTED BAND WITH JIMMY PAGE & SQUIRE
4. 1ST BAND CHANGED NAME TO THIS AFTER AMATEUR BAND CONTEST
6. ON THIS 1971 JOHN LENNON ALBUM
8. SHARED APARTMENT WITH THIS YES PRODUCER
9. ON THIS CHANT ALBUM PRODUCED BY GEORGE HARRISON
12. 1ST TIME PLAYING WITH YES WAS REHEARSING THIS SONG
13. SOLO BAND
14. POET QUOTED ON SOLO ALBUM OR DOORS NAMESAKE
15. 1ST YES ALBUM
16. CO-FOUNDED THIS GROUP WITH SHERWOOD & KAYE
20. SOLO BAND WITH 2 MEMBERS OF THIS YES TRIBUTE BAND
21. 1ST TOUR WITH YES FOR THIS ALBUM
22. REPLACED BRUFORD IN YES WHO JOINED THIS BAND
26. PART OF THIS BAND WITH KENNY CRADDOCK ORIGINALLY HAPPY MAGAZINE

PAINTING ALAN WHITE WITH NO OTHER COLORS

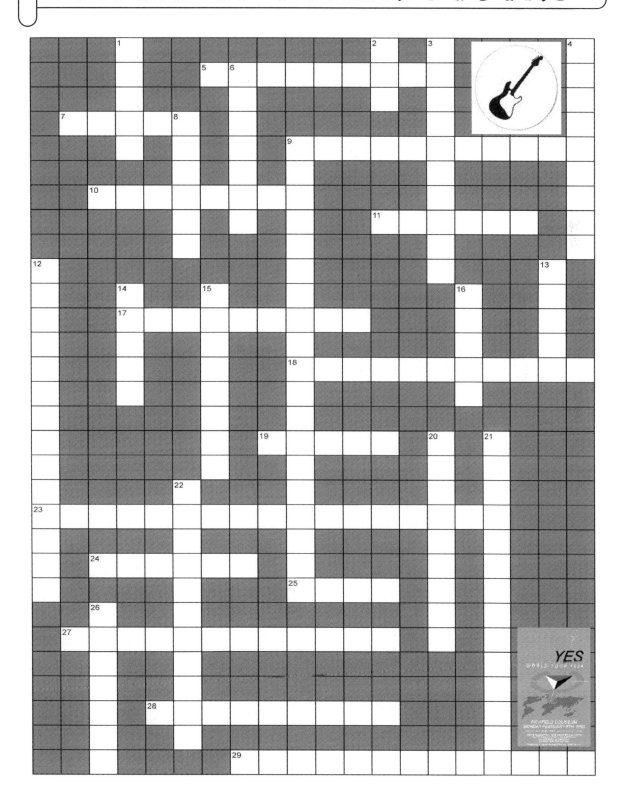

TENOR

2. TOURED WITH GENESIS FOR THIS ALBUM
4. THIS MUSIC STYLE INSPIRED LEARNING DRUMS
5. ONLY POST-RETIREMENT CONCERT WITH THIS ANN BAILEY GROUP
8. EARLY PSYCHEDELIC BAND
11. 1ST ALBUM WITH REUNITED KING CRIMSON
14. BASSIST IN KING CRIMSON WITH BRUFORD
15. PLAYED WITH THIS JAZZ FUSION BAND WITH PHIL COLLINS
16. LABEL REFUSED BAND BE FORMED WITH BRUFORD & JOHN WETTON & THIS KEYBOARDIST
20. ON THIS MORAZ SOLO ALBUM
21. BRUFORD JOBSON WETTON HOLDWORTH BAND
22. JOINED THIS PRE-YES BAND WITH ANDERSON & SQUIRE
24. 1ST BAND WHILE IN BOARDING SCHOOL OR NOT QUITE KIM DEAL GROUP
25. MEMBERS OF KING CRIMSON ON THIS ROCHES ALBUM
26. 1ST ALBUM BY RE-FORMED DOUBLE TRIO KING CRIMSON
28. HITCHHIKED TO LONDON AFTER GHASTLY ITALIAN GIG WITH THIS BAND
29. LEFT YES FOR THIS BAND

BASS

1. GROUP WITH TONY LEVIN ABBREVIATION OR MILES DAVIS KIND OF
3. LAST KING CRIMSON STUDIO ALBUM
4. HIGHLY INFLUENCED BY THIS KING CRIMSON PERCUSSIONIST
6. REUNION WITH YES ON THIS STUDIO ALBUM
7. ORIGINAL DRUMMER OF THIS CANTERBURY PROG BAND
9. FINAL STUDIO ALBUM
10. LAST ALBUM WITH YES BEFORE 1ST DEPARTURE
12. FINAL OUTING WITH KING CRIMSON VIA THIS IMPROVISATIONAL SPIN-OFF GROUP
13. 1986 JAZZ GROUP
17. SOLO DEBUT BAND
18. 2 ALBUMS WITH THIS YES KEYBOARDIST
19. 3 GIGS WITH THIS EARLY BLUES BAND WHICH HE FAILED AUDITION FOR
23. ON THIS ROY HARPER ALBUM
27. REHEARSED WITH THIS JIMMY PAGE & PAUL RODGERS GROUP

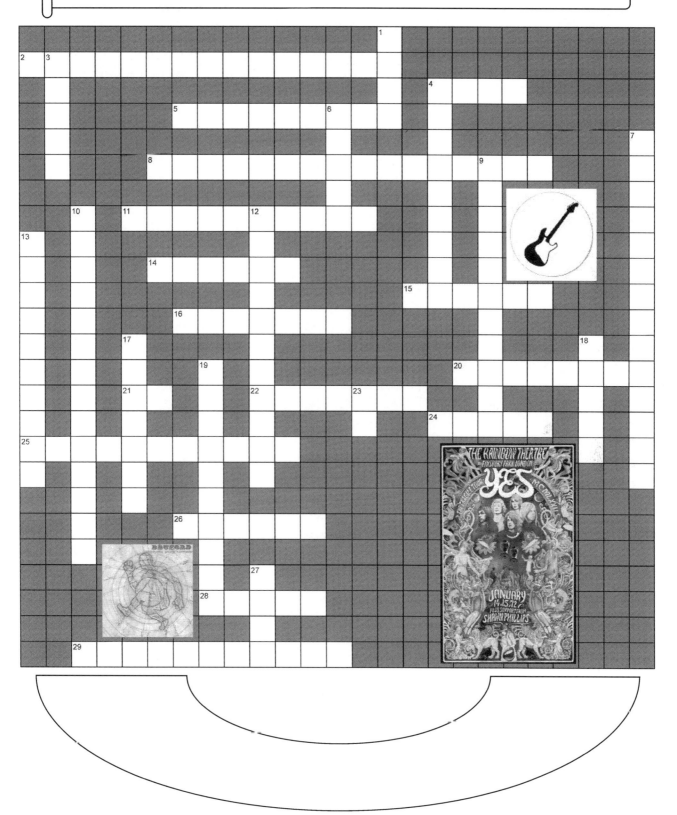

ANDERSON BRUFORD WAKEMAN HOWE

TENOR

1. 2ND LIVE ALBUM
3. *SOUND* & *SECOND ATTENTION* & *SOUL WARRIOR*
4. COVER ARTIST
6. *AN EVENING OF YES MUSIC PLUS* ALBUM COVER NAME
10. 2ND TOUR BASSIST OR GERMANY
11. *LET'S PRETEND* CO-WRITER
14. UNFINISHED 2ND STUDIO ALBUM ON THIS MULTIPLE VOL BOOTLEG COLLECTION
15. NON-ALBUM B-SIDE
19. DEMOS & TOUR GUITARIST
20. *BIRTHRIGHT* CO-WRITER OF THIS HOWE BAND
23. ONLY NON-YES MEMBER CREDITED AS SONGWRITER ON 1ST LIVE ALBUM
24. *BIRTHRIGHT* INCLUDES MUSIC WRITTEN FOR THIS BAND
25. DEMOS OF UNFINISHED 2ND STUDIO ALBUM IN THIS ANDERSON BOX SET
26. BEHIND THE SCENES TOUR FILM
28. *BROTHER OF MINE* CO-WRITER OR ASIA
29. UNFINISHED 2ND STUDIO ALBUM

BASS

2. BASSIST 2ND INSTRUMENT
3. BASSIST
5. 2ND STUDIO ALBUM FINISHED WITH THIS BAND
7. ALBUM KEYBOARDIST OR DOG
8. AN EVENING OF THIS
9. FIST OF THIS
12. AFTER SOLO SEGMENTS 1ST ABWH SONG ON BOTH LIVE ALBUMS
13. BOOTLEG ALBUM OF UNFINISHED 2ND STUDIO ALBUM
16. BRUFORD & BASSIST PREVIOUSLY IN THIS BAND
17. TOUR KEYBOARDIST
18. FOUNDING MEMBER
21. SONG REFERENCING NUMEROUS YES SONGS
22. ABWH DEMOS ON THIS HOWE SOLO ALBUM
27. 3RD PART OF *BROTHER OF MINE* BASED ON AN UNRECORDED SONG BY THIS BAND

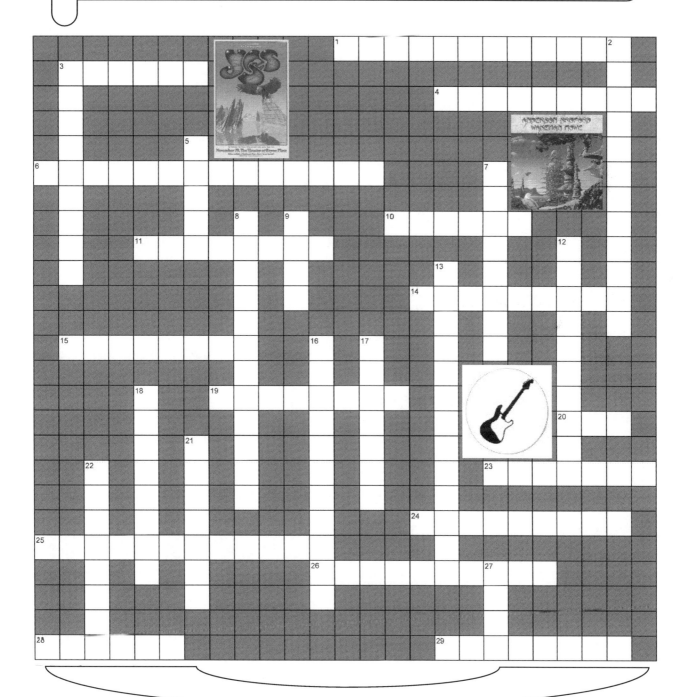

CAN YOU SAY ANDERSON BRUFORD WAKEMAN HOWE IN A SINGLE BREATHE?

TENOR

2. CIRCA ROOTED IN CHRIS SQUIRE EXPERIMENT THAT BECAME THIS
7. 2ND YOSO DRUMMER OR REED
9. YOSO STARTED AS PLANNED TOUR WITH BOBBY KIMBALL & THIS BAND
10. LAST CIRCA DRUMMER
11. YOSO & CIRCA KEYBOARDIST
12. 2 SONGS ON CIRCA DEBUT CO-WRITTEN BY THIS YES GUITARIST
17. YOSO DEBUT ALBUM
19. LUTE PLAYER ON CIRCA DEBUT OR PORTER
21. CIRCA & YOSO GUITARIST JIMMY HAUN STARTED HIS CAREER TOURING WITH THIS BANDMEMBER'S FATHER
22. 2ND CIRCA GUITARIST
24. CIRCA ORIGINAL DRUMMER
25. CIRCA LIVE VIDEO
28. YOSO ORIGINAL NAME
29. YOSO GUITARIST JOHNNY BRUHNS OF TRIBUTE BAND TO THIS GROUP OR NOT NO

BASS

1. YOSO SINGER IN THIS BAND WITH MEMBERS OF 3 DOG NIGHT
3. CIRCA BASSIST NOT SHERWOOD
4. 2ND CIRCA ALBUM
5. 3RD CIRCA GUITARIST OR STONE WOOD
6. 2ND CIRCA & ORIGINAL YOSO DRUMMER
8. YES ALBUM WITH ALL 4 ORIGINAL CIRCA MEMBERS
11. YOSO LEAD SINGER FROM THIS BAND
13. CIRCA 2011 ALBUM
14. YOSO DRUMMER SCOTT CONNOR OF TRIBUTE BAND TO THIS GROUP OR BEGINNING
15. CIRCA ALBUM IS IN THE VALLEY OF THIS OR QUIXOTE ENEMY
16. YOSO MANAGER PERFORMED IN THIS CLASSIC PROG BAND
18. YOSO FRONTMAN
20. CIRCA 2009 ALBUM
23. 1ST YOSO CONCERTS IN THIS COUNTRY
26. 3RD YOSO DRUMMER OR EXPLORER
27. WORKING NAME OF CIRCA THIS PROJECT OR WE ARE THIS

THE GEOMETRY OF YOSO & CIRCA

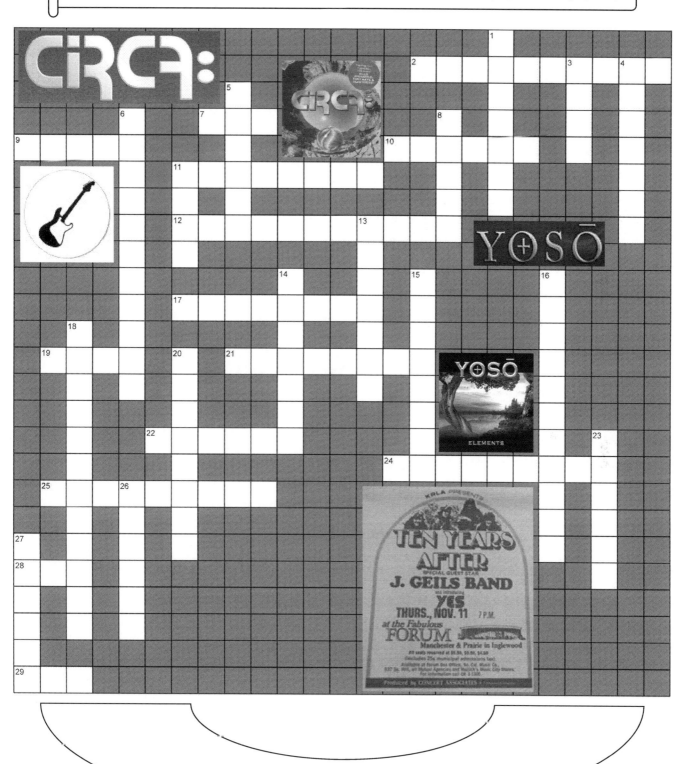

TENOR

1. BUGGLES HAVE ADVENTURES IN THESE
5. ASIA WON GRAMMY FOR THIS CATEGORY IN 1982
9. FRONTMAN OF SPLINTER ASIA GROUP
11. BUGGLES DEBUT ALBUM
14. FINAL BUGGLES SINGLE OR GINSBERG & KEROUAC
15. YES GUITARIST WHO AUDITIONED FOR ASIA
17. TENTATIVE NAME OF 3RD ASIA ALBUM
20. 2ND ASIA ALBUM
21. BUGGLES MUSIC VIDEO 1ST TO BE SHOWN ON THIS TV STATION
24. ALT VERSIONS OF 2 BUGGLES SONGS APPEARED ON ALBUM BY THIS GROUP
27. ASIA ORIGINAL LINE-UP REUNION ALBUM
28. DOWNES & HOWE POST-ASIA GROUP
29. POTENTIAL LEAD SINGER OR LIKE SAM THE SHAM

BASS

2. ORIGINAL LEAD SINGER OF ASIA OR JOURNEY'S FOR YOU
3. BEFORE ASIA JOHN WETTON IN THIS BAND WITH BRUFORD
4. 1ST BUGGLES CONCERT
6. 1ST MEMBER TO LEAVE BUGGLES
7. FILM COMPOSER WHO APPEARS IN BUGGLES VIDEO *VIDEO KILLED THE RADIO STAR*
8. WHEN ASIA CONTRIBUTED SONG TO *OVER THE TOP* MOVIE ONLY THIS ORIGINAL MEMBER IN BAND
10. GUITARIST 3RD ASIA ALBUM
12. ALBUM RELEASED WITH HORN & DOWNES IN BETWEEN BUGGLES ALBUMS
13. BUGGLES SONG *I AM A CAMERA* TIED TO THIS YES SONG
16. BUGGLES NAME INSPIRED BY THIS BAND
18. 2ND OFFICIAL ASIA DRUMMER OF THIS GROUP
19. JOHN WETTON SUCCESSOR VOCALIST
20. DOWNES CO-FOUNDED THIS BAND AFTER BUGGLES
22. BUGGLES ELECTROPOP NEW WAVE LANDMARK OF THIS MUSIC SCENE
23. 2ND BUGGLES ALBUM 1ST USE OF THIS BY HORN AS A PRODUCER
25. 1ST NON-COMP ASIA ALBUM NOT TO HAVE AN A NAME
26. JOHN WETTON IN THIS BAND BEFORE ASIA

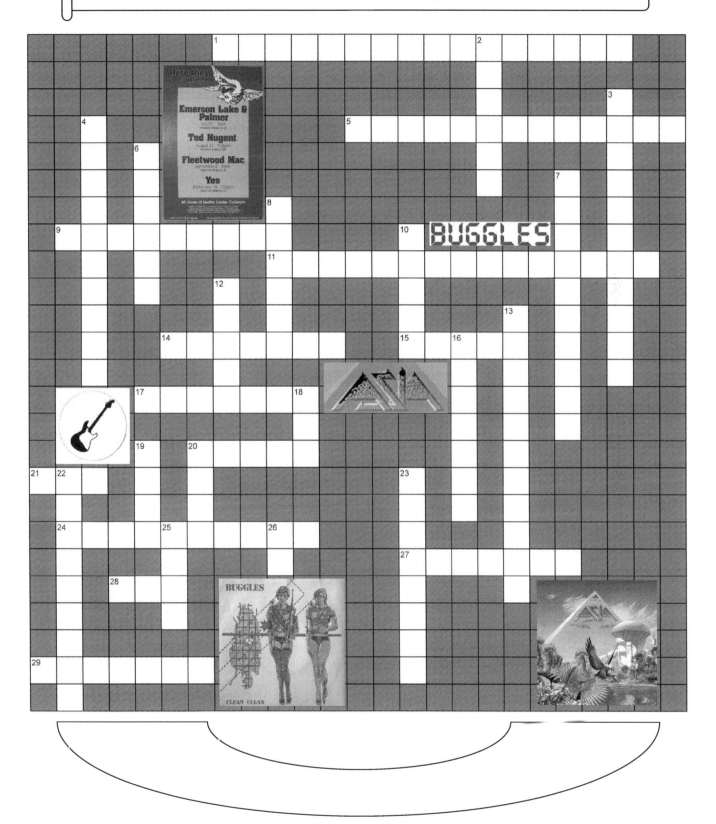

TENOR

1. EARLY VERSION OF *AWAKEN* PLAYED ON *RELAYER TOUR*
7. 1ST ANNOUNCEMENT OF ARW ON WAKEMAN RADIO SHOW
9. ONLY SONG WITH KHOROSHEV CO-WRITING CREDIT PLAYED ON TOUR
10. BYRDS SONG HEARD ON TOURS BY ORIGINAL LINE-UP
11. 1997 CANCELLED TOUR
12. ARW MEMBERS NOT TOURED TOGETHER SINCE THIS YES TOUR
18. ARW ENCORE
22. ARW TOUR BASSIST
23. OFF-STAGE KEYBOARDIST *9012LIVE TOUR* OR NOT OLD
25. 1971 PARIS SHOWS CANCELLED DUE TO THESE
26. ASIDE FROM GUITAR & VOCALS ANDERSON PLAYS THIS INSTRUMENT IN ARW
27. 5TH DIMENSION SONG HEARD ON TOURS BY ORIGINAL LINE-UP
28. BANKS FINAL PERFORMANCE WITH YES AT THIS COLLEGE
29. ARW TOUR

BASS

2. YES TOUR THAT WAS LAST FOR RABIN & 1ST WITH SHERWOOD
3. ARW CLAIMS TO HAVE THIS TYPE OF MEMBER WHICH YES DOESN'T
4. HOWE & SQUIRE SONG HEARD ON HOWE'S 1ST TOUR WITH YES
5. 1ST SHOW WITHOUT SQUIRE IN THIS STATE
6. ARW RUMORED PARTICIPANT
8. ARW CHANGED NAME TO THIS
10. BEATLES SONG PLAYED ON *9012LIVE TOUR*
13. *DRAMA* TOUR STARTED IN THIS COUNTRY
14. ARW TOUR DRUMMER
15. ARW TOUR BASSIST IN JAPAN
16. ARW TOUR NAMED IN REFERENCE TO THIS ALBUM
17. TOUR WITH HOWE PLAYING IN BOTH YES & OPENING ACT ASIA
19. ABWH SONG IN ARW SET
20. SONG ON 1ST ARW TOUR INCLUDED AS TRIBUTE TO SQUIRE OR SCHINDLERIA PRAEMATURUS
21. 1976 NORTH AMERICAN TOUR
24. ARW TOUR OPENED WITH THIS INSTRUMENTAL

ANDERSON RABIN AND WAKEMAN TOURS

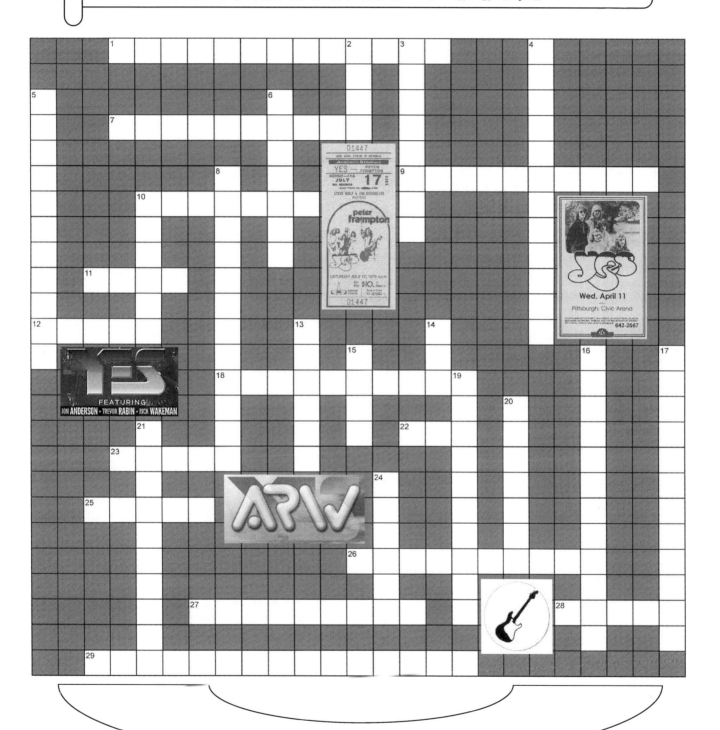

TENOR

1. 7 SHOWS FROM 1972
3. *DON'T KILL THE WHALE* FROM THIS ALBUM
6. *WALLS* FROM THIS ALBUM
7. 1ST ALBUM TO HAVE CHARTING SINGLE
9. 1ST COMP ALBUM OR BEATLES
11. *KEYS TO ASCENSION* 1 & 2
13. ALBUM WITH THE LOWEST CHARTING SINGLE
15. 1ST LIVE ALBUM
16. 2 LIVE ALBUMS
17. *SAVING MY HEART* FROM THIS ALBUM
18. YES SOLO FAMILY ALBUM
20. *SOON* ONLY SINGLE FROM THIS ALBUM
22. FINAL SQUIRE STUDIO ALBUM
23. *GOING FOR THE ONE* INCLUDES SONG ORIGINALLY MEANT FOR THIS ALBUM
25. FINAL ALBUM WITH BANKS
26. ALBUM INSPIRED BY THE BOOK *AUTOBIOGRAPHY OF A YOGI*
27. ANDERSON LEFT 2ND TIME AFTER TOURING THIS ALBUM
28. HIGHEST CHARTING U.S. ALBUM
29. HOUSE OF BLUES LIVE ALBUM

BASS

2. 2ND LIVE ALBUM
4. LOWEST CHARTING U.S. ALBUM
5. DOWNES RETURNED TO YES WITH THIS ALBUM
8. 1ST ALBUM WITH SHERWOOD AS OFFICIAL MEMBER
10. WAKEMAN RETURNED 1ST TIME WITH THIS ALBUM
12. 1994 - 2001 ALBUMS BOX SET
14. DEBUT ALBUM
19. ALBUM OF YES MUSIC REMIXED BY VIRGIL HOWE
21. COMPANION ALBUM TO BOX SET *IN A WORD*
24. 1ST ALBUM WITH WAKEMAN
26. 1ST ALBUM WITH KHOROSHEV AS OFFICIAL MEMBER

COLLECTING ALBUMS

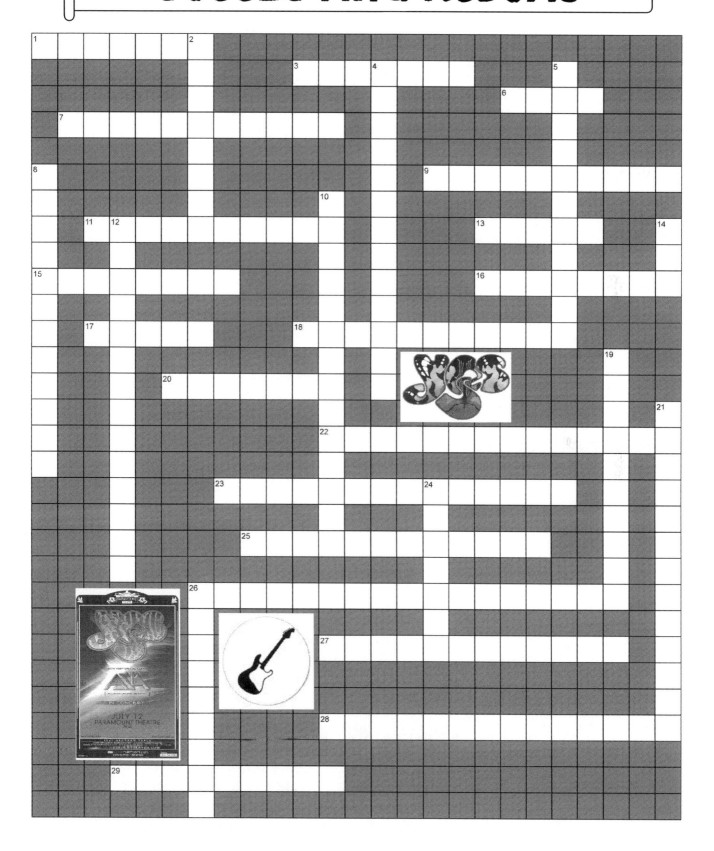

TENOR

1. SONG INCLUDING *DAY TRIPPER* RIFF
4. ONLY SONG ON *YESTERDAYS* COMP WITHOUT BANKS
7. ONLY SINGLE WITH DOWNES
10. *CIRCUS OF HEAVEN* FROM *TORMATO* ALBUM INSPIRED BY THIS FANTASY WRITER
11. 7 PART SONG ON *KEYS TO ASCENSION*
15. ALT VERSION OF SINGLE RELEASED YEAR LATER BY BUGGLES
16. 2ND SINGLE ON *UNION* RELEASED AFTER SINGLE FROM THIS ALBUM
20. HIGHEST CHARTING PRE-RABIN SINGLE ANYWHERE IN THE WORLD
24. BETWEEN 1971 - 1997 ONLY STUDIO SINGLE NOT TO CHART
25. UNCREDITED KEYBOARDIST ON *YESTERDAYS* COMP
27. NOVELIST INSPIRING *CLOSE TO THE EDGE*
28. WAKEMAN INTRO ON *CHILDREN OF LIGHT* MIXED OUT OF ORIGINAL ALBUM
29. 1ST CHARTING SINGLE ANYWHERE IN THE WORLD
30. SONG FROM *THE YES ALBUM* NOT PLAYED LIVE UNTIL 2013

BASS

2. 1ST ALBUM TO FEATURE A CHARTING SINGLE
3. 2ND ALBUM TO HAVE 2 CHARTING SINGLES
5. *CAN YOU SEE* FROM XYZ PROJECT WITH JIMMY PAGE BECAME THIS ON *MAGNIFICATION*
6. SINGLE RELEASED IN 1972 & THEN AS LIVE VERSION IN 1973
8. YES SONG FROM XYZ PROJECT WITH JIMMY PAGE
9. SONG WRITTEN BY ANDERSON & VANGELIS
12. SONG NAMED AFTER SAX PLAYER
13. FINAL SINGLE FROM *90125*
14. CO-WRITER OF *WALLS* FROM *TALK* ALBUM FROM THIS BAND
17. 1ST SINGLE
18. SONG CREDITED ONLY TO DAVISON ON *HEAVEN & EARTH*
19. ONLY SONG ON *YESYEARS* COMP TO INCLUDE SHERWOOD
21. HIGHEST CHARTING SINGLE FROM *TALK*
22. FROM 1980 - 2010 ONLY STUDIO ALBUM TO HAVE ONLY ONE SINGLE RELEASED
23. ONLY SONG ON *BIG GENERATOR* WITHOUT RABIN CO-WRITING CREDIT
26. AFTER SINGLES BEGAN CHARTING 1ST ALBUM NOT TO HAVE CHARTING SINGLE

SO MANY SONGS

MABEL GREER'S TOYSHOP & THE SYN

ADELMAN   ALANWHITE   ARMISTICEDAY   ATLANTIC   BANKS   BARRE
BEYONDANDBEFORE   BIGSKY   BILL   BILLY   CHRIS   CLIVE   GUN
HAGGER   HIGHCOURT   IMAGES   JACKMAN   JIMI   JON   KAYE   LONDON
MABELGREER   MOREDRAMA   NARDELLI   NEATCHANGE   NEWWAYOFLIFE
NOISE   PAINTER   PAUL   PEEL   PETER   SELFS   STACEY   SWEETNESS
SYN   SYNDESTRUCTIBLE   THEROOTSOFYES   TIMEANDAWORD   WETTON
WHITE

SQUIRE

ABWH   ALIENS   ALIFEWITHINADAY   ASTEROID   BILL   CHEMISTRY
CHURCH   CLOSETOTHEEDGE   CONSPIRACY   ESQUIRE   FINALLY   FISH
GRAHAM   HACKETT   HOLDOUTYOURHAND   ICANTEXPLAIN   LEUKEMIA
MELISSA   MORAZ   NIKKI   OPENYOUREYES   RICKENBACKER   SCOTLAND
SELFS   SHERWOOD   SWISSCHOIR   SYN   THEFISH   WHITE   XYZ

SHERWOOD & WAKEMAN

ANDERSON   BENOIT   CLASSICROCK   CONSPIRACY   CROSSFIRE   DOWNES
DRAGONATTACK   ENGINEER   EXPERIMENT   FLYFROMHERE   GILTRAP
HAUN   HEAVENSISLE   HOUSEOFYES   INTHEPRESENT   JABBERWOCKY
JAY   JEFFOLOGY   JON   LODGIC   LYON   MAGICK   MILTONBERLE
MOTHERSRUIN   OPENYOUREYES   PALJOEY   PETERBANKS   POEMS
POLAND   RITEOFSPRING   SPECTRUM   SQUIRE   STARCASTLE   STRAWBS
TALK   THEBIGPEACE   THEHUMANEQUATION   TOTO   UNION   WORLDTRADE

ANDERSON

APB   CHAGALL   CINEMA   CIRCUSOFHEAVEN   DESEO   DIALOGUE   DRAMA
DREAM   EARTHMOTHEREARTH   FROMMETOYOU   GLASSHAMMER
HANSCHRISTIAN   JONES   MAGNIFICATION   METROPOLIS   NAPOLEON
NEWLIFE   OLIAS   OPEN   RICK   STOLT   THEDESEOREMIXES
THELIVINGTREE   THELOSTTAPES   THEPROMISERING   TOLTEC   TOTO
VANGELIS   WARRIORS   YOUCAMEALONG

DAVID & DAVISON

ANDERSON   BAKER   BUGGLES   CHURCH   CITIZEN   CLOSETOTHEEDGE
DOWNES   EARTH   FLYFROMHERE   FOOFIGHTERS   FRANCE
GLASSHAMMER   HAMADRYAD   HORN   INTHEPRESENT   JUANO
LIKEITIS   MACHINEMESSIAH   MAGNIFICATION   MESAARTSCENTER
MYSTERY   OLIVER   PROGENY   QUEBEC   RONALD   ROUNDABOUT
SKYCRIESMARY   SQUIRE   THESAMURAIOFPROG   WAKEMAN

RABIN

ASIA BEGINNINGS BLUECHIPMUSIC BOYSWILLBEBOYS BRUCE
CANTLOOKAWAY CINEMA CONDUCTOR CONGLOMERATION DRUMS
FACETOFACE FOREIGNER JACARANDAROOM JETHROTULL LIVEINLA
MANFREDMANN OTHER PIANO RAYDAVIES SARIE SEGAL
SOULPATROL SOUTHAFRICA SUPERTRAMP TALK THEGLIMMERMAN
TREVORRABIN VIOLIN WILDHORSE WOLF

HOWE

AQUA ASIA BANKS BEGINNINGS BLOCKHEADS BODAST CLASSICAL
DRAMA DYLAN GIBSON GTR GUITARPLAYER HOMEBREW INCROWD
INNUENDO KEYSTOASCENSION LITTLEBARRIE LOUREED MAYBELLENE
NICE PATRICK PHOENIX STEVEHOWETRIO SYMPHONICMUSIC
SYNDICATS THEYESALBUM TIMEANDAWORD TOMORROW UNION
VEGETARIAN

BANKS & KHOROSHEV

BILLY BLODWYNPIG BROCKBANKS CAKEWALK COWBELL
DEVILSDISCIPLES ELP EMPIRE FAIRBAIRN FENWICK FLASH HELLO
HOMEWORLD HOUSEOFYES JOEPERRYPROJECT LOVEKARMA
MABELGREERSTOYSHOP MARLEY NIGHTHAWKS OPENYOUREYES
PIANOWORKS SHERWOOD SOMETHINGSCOMING SYNDICATS THELADDER
THESYN TIMEANDAWORD TRUEYOUTRUEME YARDBIRDS YES

WAKEMAN

AIRS BIROTRON BOWIE CHELSEA DALI EARTH FRAGILE
FRAGILECARRIAGE GRUMPYOLDPICTURE HENRYVIII HERITAGESUITE
KINGARTHUR LIGHTUPTHESKY LOUREED LUREOFTHEWILD
NOEARTHLY OLIVER ONETAKE OZZMOSIS PEEL PERIVALE
ROCKNROLLPROPHET SABBRACADDABRA SAYYES SIMPLYACOUSTIC
SOFTSWORD SUNTRILOGY THELIVINGTREE TURNER VIBRATIONS

KAYE

BADFINGER BADGER BONZO BOOTHILL BOWIE CINEMA CIRCA
DETECTIVE FEDERALS FLASH FRAGILE HALLYDAY HAMMOND HAUN
JAZZ JOBSON KEYBOARD MANAGEMENT RABIN ROYALTIES SI
SQUIRE STATIONTOSTATION TALK THENEILDEAL THISISSPINALTAP
TOYSHOP WAKEMAN YOSO YOURSISNODISGRACE

DOWNES & HORN

ARMENIA   ARTOFNOISE   ASIA   BASS   BIGGENERATOR   BRAIDE
CHROMIUM   COMEDANCING   COULDITBEMAGIC   DRAMA
FLOWERSINTHEDIRT   FLYFROMHERE   ICON   IDOL   ISLAND   JINGLES
LANE   NEWDANCE   NUMAN   PERFECTSONGS   PRODUCERS   RELAX
SHESFRENCH   STARTOSTAR   TATU   THEBIGA   THEOUTERLIMITS
TINACHARLES   TRAPEZE   WHITE

MORAZ

BALLET   BEGINNINGS   BILLBRUFORD   CHAT   COLTRANE   DALI   ESP
FISHOUTOFWATER   GOINGFORTHEONE   GOLD   GRAPPELLI
KEYSOFTHEKINGDOM   MAINHORSE   OCTAVE   OUTINTHESUN   PADEREWSKI
PIANISSIMORAZ   PREDATOR   REFUGEE   RELAYER   RICK   SCUBADIVING
SWITZERLAND   THESALAMANDER   THESPIRIT   THESTORYOFI   VANGELIS
VIMANA   WINDOWSOFTIME   ZURICH

WHITE

ALLTHINGSMUSTPASS   ARCHITECTURE   BALLS   BILLYFURY   BLAKE
BLUECHIPS   BUD   CIRCA   CLOSETOTHEEDGE   DOWNBEATS   ERIC
GINGER   GRIFFIN   IMAGINE   KINGCRIMSON   LIVEPEACE   MORAZ
MYBONNIE   OFFORD   PARALLELS   PIANO   RAMSHACKLED
RUNWITHTHEFOX   SIBERIANKHATRU   THERADHAKRSNATEMPLE   THESYN
TOPOGRAPHIC   WHITE   XYZPROJECT   YESSONGS

BRUFORD

ATRICKOFTHETAIL   BLUE   BRANDX   BREED   BRUFORD
CLOSETOTHEEDGE   DISCIPLINE   EARTHWORKS   FIRM   HQ   JAMIEMUIR
JAZZ   KEEPONDOING   KINGCRIMSON   MORAZ   NATIONALHEALTH   NOISE
PAPERBLITZTISSUE   PROJEKCTONE   SAVOYBROWN   SKINANDWIRE
SOULHOUSE   THRAK   TIMECODE   TOYSHOP   UK   UNION   VROOOM
WAKEMAN   WETTON

ABWH

ANDERSON   ASIA   BERLIN   BIRTHRIGHT   BRITTEN   CHAPMANSTICK
CLIFFORD   COLBECK   DIALOGUE   DOWNES   FIRE   FLOATINGISLAND   GTR
HOMEBREW   KINGCRIMSON   LIVEATTHENEC   MCDONALD   NEROTREND
OFFTHEWALL   QUARTET   ROGERDEAN   THELOSTTAPES   THEMES
TONYLEVIN   UNION   VANGELIS   VULTURES   WEMAKEBELIEVE
YESMUSICPLUS   YESOTERIC

YOSO & CIRCA

AKA ALANWHITE ANDSOON BOBBYKIMBALL BRUHNS CIRCA
CIRCAHQ CIRCALIVE COLE CONNOR CONSPIRACY CORTEZ ELEMENTS
FAMILY GENESIS GENTLEGIANT JAYSCHELLEN LOU MEXICO
OVERFLOW RICK RONNIE SHERWOOD SSFOOLS TONYKAYE TOTO
TREVORRABIN UNION WINDMILL YES

BUGGLES & ASIA

AHA ALPHA ARCADIA ASIA BEATLES BEATNIK BESTNEWARTIST
CAMERACLUB DOWNES DRAMA GTR HANSZIMMER INTOTHELENS
JOHNPAYNE KINGCRIMSON LAKE MEYER MODERNRECORDINGS MTV
PHOENIX RABIN RARE ROBERT SAMPLING TECHNOPOP
THEAGEOFPLASTIC THELOSTGIG UK WETTON WOOLLEY

ARW & TOURS

ABASSODYSSEY BRUFORD CANADA CARPETMAN CELTICHARP CINEMA
CONNECTICUT HIGHVIBRATION IAIN IMDOWN INTHEPRESENT
ISEEYOU KNOW LEE LOU LUTON NINEVOICES ORIGINAL
PLANETROCK RIOTS ROUNDABOUT SOLOALBUMS TALK THEFISH
THEMEETING UNION YESFEATURING YESMUSICANDMORE
YESMUSICPLUS YOUNG

ALBUMS

AFFIRMATIVE BIGGENERATOR CLOSETOTHEEDGE DRAMA
ESSENTIALLYYES FISHOUTOFWATER FLYFROMHERE FRAGILE
GOINGFORTHEONE HEAVENANDEARTH HUSEOFYES KEYSSTUDIO
LIKEITIS MAGNIFICATION OPENYOUREYES PROGENY RELAYER TALK
THELADDER THEWORDISLIVE THEYESALBUM TIMEANDAWORD
TOPOGRAPHICOCEANS TORMATO UNION YES YESREMIXES YESSHOWS
YESSONGS YESTERDAYS

SONGS

AMERICA AVENTURE BRUFORD CANYOUIMAGINE CHILDRENOFLIGHT
EVERYLITTLETHING GOINGFORTHEONE HAROLDLAND HESSE HOLDON
HOLYLAMB INTOTHELENS LIGHTNING LIGHTOFTHEAGES
LOVECONQUERSALL MINDDRIVE OPENYOUREYES RAY RELAYER
ROUNDABOUT SOON SUPERTRAMP SWEETNESS THATTHATIS
THECALLING THEYESALBUM WECANFLY WONDEROUSSTORIES
YESYEARS YOURMOVE

CODA

**THANKS FOR PICKING UP THIS LITTLE PUZZLE BOOK.
NOW CHECK OUT THE OTHER BOOKS BY AARON JOY.**

(SERIES 5)   KRAUTROCK ... ROCK KEYBOARDISTS ... ROCK PIANISTS
PIANISTS & KEYBOARDISTS OMNIBUS ... DUB ... YES FAMILY TREE

(SERIES 4)   REGGAE ... MOD ... JAZZ ROCK ... BRITISH BLUES PIONEERS
CANADIANS SOUTH OF THE BORDER ... LED ZEPPELIN FAMILY TREE

(SERIES 3)   DRONE METAL ... CANTERBURY PROG ROCK ... BOY BANDS
CLASSIC SURF BANDS ... EARLY CHRISTIAN ROCK & JESUS MUSIC

(SERIES 2)   BOSTON BANDS ... GAY MUSICIANS ... LESBIAN MUSICIANS
GAY & LESBIAN MUSICIANS OMNIBUS ... SLUDGE METAL

(SERIES 1)   THRASH ... WOMEN THAT ROCK ... PROG ROCK ... GRUNGE
L.A. HAIR METAL ... NYC CLASSIC ROCK BANDS

(BLUES SERIES)   HARMONICA PLAYERS ... PIEDMONT BLUES

(RAP SERIES)   MUMBLE RAP

(FOLK SERIES)   UKULELE

(PRESIDENTIAL SERIES)   LIBERTARIAN PRESIDENTIAL CANDIDATES
FREEMASON PRESIDENTS & VICE-PRESIDENTS

(THEATER SERIES)   LESBIAN PLAYWRIGHTS

* * * * *

(NON-CROSSWORD MUSIC BOOKS)
HEAVY METAL MUSIC FROM THE INSIDE: QUOTES ON BEING A ROCKER

THE PIANOS I HAVE KNOWN:
THE AUTOBIOGRAPHY OF IRVING FIELDS

**SMALL PRINT: NO ONE FEATURED IN THESE PUZZLES
HAVE ENDORSED NOR ARE INVOLVED IN THEIR
CREATION NOR RECEIVE ANY FINANCIAL STIPEND.
THIS IS A TRIBUTE BY A MUSICIAN & MUSIC LOVER.**

Made in United States
Orlando, FL
22 January 2022